LOVE.
LOVE.
LOVE.

a collection of mindfulness poetry

Kim Nicole

Copyright © 2023 Kim Nicole

All rights reserved. This book or any portion thereof may not be reproduced or used in any manner whatsoever without the express written permission of the publisher except for the use of brief quotations in a book review.

ISBN

E-Book: 979-8-89184-949-5

Paperback: 979-8-89184-947-1

Hardback: 979-8-89184-948-8

Acknowledgment

This is my first acknowledgment. Attempting to convey the perfect words of gratitude, I have decided it does not have to be perfect. Just in the moment, and from my heart.

Have you ever had a chance encounter in which you were awestruck? That immediate energy you felt was filled with kindness! A familiarity of knowing this person from another lifetime. Their smile conveyed a celebration. Wishing you eternal happiness.

Some of those encounters for me have evolved into lifelong friendships having a profound impact on my life.

I have eternal gratitude to those individuals.

Thank you for your kindness.
Thank you for your wisdom.
Thank you for your truth.
Thank you for having the courage to be you.
Thank you for your laughter and silliness in a world that can often be too rigid.

To my soul sisters, my mentors, my spiritual family, and Cheeky.

To the most beautiful soul, Fluffy Buffy, always and forever with you.

I love you all!

LOVE. LOVE. LOVE.

a collection of mindfulness poetry

To love is to
be kind

To love is to have
compassion

To love is to speak
your truth

For this is the path I have chosen to live.

Created by
Kim Nicole

Introduction

The experience of mindfulness poetry is kind, inspiring, truthful, and compassionate. Not just mere words but language carefully selected to evoke a quiet introspection into our true nature. Our Buddha nature.

Creating, flourishing, and loving on a profound level.

We are awakened to a new journey.

For all Beings seeking to live fully in each moment, may you be inspired and connect with your heart.

With loving kindness and gratitude to you,

Kim Nicole

Table of Contents

Chapter 1: Loving Kindness 2
    Loving Kindness 3
    Just as I Wish To 4
Chapter 2: The Practice of Simply Being 6
    My Mindfulness 7
    Dear Beautiful Self 9
    Liberated from Permanence 10
    Truth Be Told 12
    Sati 14
    Do Not Look Away 15
Chapter 3: Wise Speech 18
    Wise Speech 19
Chapter 4: A Single Breath 21
    When I Take a Breath 22
    To Take a Breath 23
Chapter 5: RAIN 26
    This Too I Can Hold 27
Chapter 6: A Formal Practice 29
    Impermanence 30
    My Meditation This Morning 31
Chapter 7: Our Mother Earth 34
    Wildflower 35
    Remembering You 36
Chapter 8: Deeply Heard, Deeply Seen 39
    To Be Deeply Heard 40

This wall 42
Chapter 9: The Intimacy of Love 44
   My Heart is a Little Bit Broken 45
   If You Only Knew 47
   The Mirroring of Our Souls 48
   True Love 50
   When Our Souls Met 51
   A Quiet Heart 52
Chapter 10: True Beauty is Flawless 54
   Can you see me? 55
   Illusions of the Face 56
Chapter 11: The Mindfulness of Children 60
   Children: Living Life in This Moment 61
   Children: Living Life in This Moment 62
Chapter 12: The Joy of Writing 64
   Just like Poetry 65
   Knowing 66
   As Life Unfolds 67
   Dedication 69
   Who is Kim Nicole 70

Chapter 1: Loving Kindness

To wish for unconditional love.
May you be blessed.

Loving Kindness

Freedom from harm and all that does not serve your Divine self.
This is what I wish for you.

To be embraced and held with loving kindness, joy, and happiness.
This is what I wish for you.

A healthy mind so you may speak your truth.
A healthy body singing to your unique rhythm.
A healthy soul awakening your true essence.
This is what I wish for you.

Peace and serenity with every breath.
This is what I wish for you.

In this moment, my heart celebrates only thoughts of loving kindness for you.

Just as I Wish To

Next time you witness your neighbor struggling,
quietly whisper…

Just as I wish to,
May you be safe.
May you be healthy.
May you live with ease and happiness.

Chapter 2: The Practice of Simply Being

Existing in this moment is our only truth.

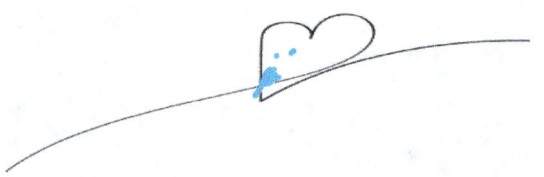

My Mindfulness

I began my practice of mindfulness believing this beautiful journey would gift me eternal happiness & contentment. Instill within me a wisdom, a knowingness to answer all of life's challenges. I would finally be whole. Be seen. My voice deeply heard and respected.

In this moment sharing with you, I do not feel content. I do not feel at peace. I do not feel seen or heard. I cannot answer questions to all of life's challenges. I am in the shadows of darkness where respect is unseen.

I am here feeling wounded and vulnerable. I am here filled with sadness. I am here feeling more confused.

My identities and images of self that I held onto for so long, no longer feel true. I do not find comfort in them. My foundation is crumbling, fading away into non-existence.

I cannot pretend to BE any longer.

I am changing.
Seeing differently.
Feeling like I have never felt before.

My soul is raw, lost in an emptiness.
My breath holds me down like an anchor.
I do not know who I am.

What am I supposed to do?

Aah…

Let go.
Let go of self.
Let go of expectations.
Let go of all that is not my True Nature.

I feel a sadness and fear as I let go.

My heart gently whispers to me… "I am with you."

As I take refuge in my heart, the warmth of loving kindness and self- compassion flows through me like a beautiful ocean wave. I am seeing myself for the first time with all my wounds and my joy.

My long-time companion, Judgment, tells me "I cannot continue this journey with you anymore."

I exhale and let go.
For some reason, I do not feel abandoned.

In this moment, that is the only way I can exist.
Not chained to the past or lost in the future.

I am here with you.
Pausing together.
Embracing each other's existence.
Bearing witness to each other's suffering without judgment and with compassion.

To just exist in the moment.

Dear Beautiful Self

Dear Beautiful Self,

I cannot promise
perfect ease and simplicity in this lifetime.

I cannot promise
an endless flow of happiness.

I cannot promise
your relationships in this moment will be present tomorrow.

I cannot promise
suffering and pain will not cross your path.

I do promise
a discovery of self not in alignment with attachment, grasping, and desire.

I do promise
existing in this moment will reveal glimpses of your true and pure nature.

I do promise
honoring the stillness within you will awaken a gentle smile remembering… "I am my breath."

I do promise
a return to compassion, loving kindness, and warmth of being.

Your Beloved,

Mindfulness

Liberated from Permanence

Every wakeful moment has been tormented with angst.

Struggling to simply keep abreast.

Beneath my skin are layers of pain and confusion.

I am drowning deep into despair.
Far reaching the ocean's abyss.

My heart broken.

Crushed.
Stomped.
Chewed up and spit out with no consequence to you.

What can I do? I do not know.
I believe it to be ok not to know.

Permanence is not promised to me.

Am I purely light and joy?

No.

I am my dark shadow in this moment.
A shadow that is refusing to hide itself.

It is dominating me.
Overwhelming and suffocating.

Endless joy is not promised to me.

Leaning into you.
Embracing you.
I refuse to hide from my darkness.

It receives me with compassion and a kind curiosity.

Whispering to me that this too is temporary.
I am not alone.

Truth extends its hand.
Hold tight.
Telling me this is a part of my journey.

It is beautiful and promising.
Full of hope and love.

A calling to renounce all which does not serve my highest self.

Let go… let go… let go… let go…

I am alive with every emotion, feeling, and thought.

Liberated from permanence.

Truth Be Told

Truth be told, I am not living my truth.

I am an act.
I am an illusion.
I am not who you think I am.

How could you know my truth? I have only shown
you layers of false personas and constructed images.

Truth be told,
I do not understand why I disclose to you.
Share with me.
Who are you?
What is your truth?

I will bare my soul and heart to you.
Truth be told, this is my truth.

It is undeniable how much I love you.
Despite your harsh edges, I see past your false
personas and constructed images you have worked
so hard to craft.

Never judging. My heart yearns for you.
Patiently awaiting your return home.
You could not hide your true nature from me for I am
you.

How I remember you now!
So vividly!

You have always known me.
Your loving kindness soars within me.

My heart pounding like 10,000 peoples marching to victory!

Your truth is liberating.
I am weeping wildly, uncontrollably.
Please forgive me for abandoning you.

No words to be spoken as you greet my tears with a gentle smile.

The guilt and shame embraced by your kindness and compassion.
Never bitter.

Truth be told,
I am grateful for your serenity and gentleness in this moment.

I am the absolute truth.

I am you.

SATI

A gentle knowing.

I gaze upon you with delight.

I cannot help but smile.

Your soul is the kindest.

I adore you.

How beautiful and radiant I feel in your presence.
You and I in this moment.

Fully aware.

A perfect harmony.

Do Not Look Away

I try to connect with you.
My eyes wide open with anticipation.
I look in your direction as we approach each other.
I hold my gaze, but you look away.
Sometimes, you do not even acknowledge me.
Your attention attached to your phone.
Or some other worldly distraction.

I feel odd. Out of place.
Have I done something wrong by looking upon you
with a gentle smile and wonder?

Are we not the same?
Born from our mother's womb of love and
compassion.

Pause...

Just you and me alone in this space.

Determined.
Stubborn.
Not to make a connection.
Your pride is baffling to me.

A hint of hope that you may notice me.

No.

You leave me alone.
Never looking back.

Chapter 3:
Wise Speech

If only to pause. Aware of our impact. Embracing each other with kindness and truth.

The power of words.

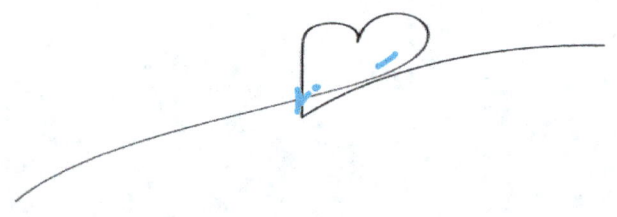

WISE SPEECH

My anger is soaring.
I witness your rage.
The tone in your voice is cruel. I counter with callousness.

Harming each other's spirit.
Surrendering to fear. Surrendering to ego.
This path we tread is familiar.
Suffering. Chaotic.

This is what we choose? To be anchored to our pain.

No!

Help me to understand your pain.
I want to know your heart. I want to see your soul.
Deeply listening to you in this moment with
kindness, compassion, and absence of judgment.

Can you feel that?

Truth.
Wisdom.
Love.

Chapter 4:
A Single Breath

To let go of all that does not serve your highest self,

this is what our breath can achieve.

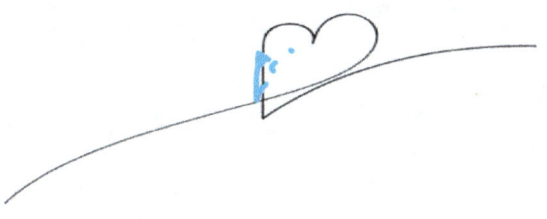

When I Take a Breath

I take a breath,
a gentle smile is awakened.

I take a breath,
my mind, body & soul dance as one.

I take a breath,
my heart embraces suffering & joy with the strength
of a lion's roar.

I take a breath,
I am simply a reflection of all that is you.

I take a breath,
wisdom, love, compassion welcome me home.

To Take a Breath

Angst, fear, & worry bound me.
To take a breath…

My body, spirit, and soul are exhausted.
To take a breath…

Overwhelmed with thought and emotion.
To take a breath…

Uncertain of my future.
To take a breath…

I sit in stillness.
Alone.
Looking into your eyes.
Leaning towards you without hesitation.
I take a breath….

Compassion, loving kindness, and curiosity welcome my frail self.
I take a breath…

Dissipating into emptiness.
I take a breath…

Angst, fear, and worry desert me.
These emotions are so fickle.
They will return.
I take a breath…

No longer manipulated by suffering.
I take a breath…

Chapter 5: Rain

I lean into all that arises within.
For I am not alone.
My companions, compassion, and love, always hold me with comfort and ease.

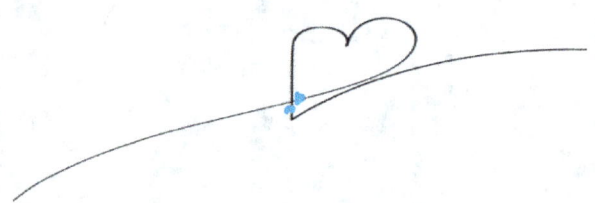

This Too I Can Hold

A deep curiosity arises as I study my reflection in the mirror. Glaring back at me are fear, anger, sadness, undeserving, shame, and uncertainty.

My eyes wide open, unable to turn away from my monkey mind. Tears saturating my face.

I am overwhelmed.

Staring at my dark shadows is taking all the breath I have in this moment.

I will not look away.
Choosing to lean into this murky space that I often run from. Recognizing this is my grief staring back at me.

Kindness holds my hand allowing me to be fully present in this moment with all that surfaces.

I cannot be here alone.
I call upon compassion and no judgment to stand beside me as I investigate the thoughts, feelings, and stories playing around in my mind.

Remembering my breath. My beautiful anchor. My sacred space. I begin to nurture myself.

Feeling liberated.
My Buddha nature whispers to me.

This too I can hold.

Chapter 6:
A Formal Practice

A commitment to my mindfulness and meditation practice without attachment to perfection.

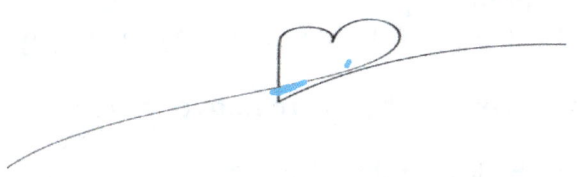

Impermanence

I have been struggling these days.

My mind ridden with worry.
My body entangled with anxiety.
My breath faint and unavailable to me.

I lay awake last night tormenting myself with endless thoughts.

Thinking.
Thinking.
Thinking.

As dawn approached,
Impermanence spoke to me…

In these moments,
you may struggle but you are not your struggle.

You may worry but you are not your worry.

You may be lost without breath.
Your breath will never leave you.

My Meditation This Morning

Nestled between two comfy cushions.

A Himalayan salt lamp is illuminating the room.

I close my eyes.

Feeling the seat beneath me as I rock back and forth; adjusting my posture until it feels just right.

My feet reach towards the ground.
My toes spread apart grasping the cold stone floor.

My hands cup each other but not too tight. Embracing each finger like a pattern in a puzzle.

I am becoming attuned to the sounds happening. Air condition blowing, birds chatting outside my window, traffic passing on the street below.

The rise and fall of my belly is my breath today. My anchor.

Counting at first... one breath in... one breath out... until I am lost. No longer counting and just existing.

Thinking.
Thinking. Thinking.
Thinking. Thinking. Thinking.
Calm of thoughts.
Thinking. Thinking. Thinking. Thinking.
Thinking.
Calm of thoughts.

Compassion.
Loving Kindness.
Curiosity.
No judgment.
Celebrating my awareness of the thinking mind.

Seeing it.
Naming it.
Gently let go.

Returning to this moment.
The rise and fall of my belly.
My breath. My anchor.

Keep returning.
Keep returning.
Keep returning.
Keep returning.

This is my meditation today.

Chapter 7:
Our Mother Earth

Nature continues to thrive despite the chaos of our world. A beautiful reminder of hope.

Wildflower

Standing statuesque in a field of grass.
Hues of green with lofty ornamental blades embracing all that exists.

Follow the sunlight. Her rays are kissing me with glee.

I am a wildflower in full bloom.
Hints of yellow, pink, red, purple, and blue wildly illuminating my mother's earth.

My petals gently sway in a dance with nature's breath.

Tender and untamed in this moment.
Freedom to be.

Gaze upon me.
Can you feel your heart beating with wondrous emotion and hope?

I am Divine. Inspired. Heavenly.
Such wild beauty.

I am what I believe.

A wildflower in full bloom

Remembering You

I was not looking for you.
Walking unaware. Not in the present moment.
Until I gazed upon you.

Alone purposely.
There you sat in your cage.

The others were housed in twos.
But you…. sitting there with your big brown eyes.
I felt suffering.
You have lived.

My heart opened to you.
A deep knowing.
You and I belong to each other.
A familiar love.

A beautiful life we celebrated together.
So much happiness you brought into my existence.

Now I mourn.
Tears well up in my eyes.
You have left me without notice.

I miss you.

A faint whisper comforts me.
I know it is you.

You will always be with me.
You have never left me.

I love you.

I love you.
I love you.

Cheeky, my furry friend.

Chapter 8:
Deeply Heard, Deeply Seen

To be listened to beyond the chaotic noise of chatter.
To be seen beneath the superficial
layers are all anyone wants.

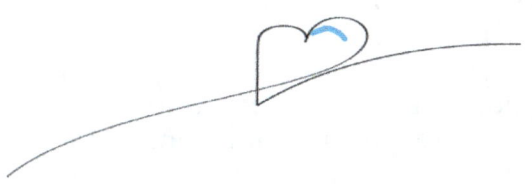

To Be Deeply Heard

Captive for all its life.
I can feel my voice fighting to escape.

No more… No more… No more.

It takes flight into this world.
Breaking away from what is expected.

Pushing its way into the open.
To be deeply seen by the light.

Unbinding itself from the entanglements of opinions,
a need to please and be docile.

Unfolding into a flow of authentic, raw vulnerability.

My voice is liberated.
My voice breathes.

Singing notes of truth and emotion.
It does not retreat from conflict but welcomes it with wise speech.

Aww... a slow, steady, and tranquil breath….
To be deeply heard, one must listen closely to their own voice.

Respect it.
Hold it with compassion and kindness.
Set it free.

For this is your only voice.

This Wall

This wall stands so tall.
A boundary between you and me.

Suffocating.
Refusing any movement forward.

An uneasiness prevails.
I know this feeling.
It has led to a broken humanity.

Why?

Fear of not being deeply seen… deeply heard…
deeply understood.

What if we began to tear down this wall?

Respect.
Hope.
Love.

Pause……….

Chapter 9: The Intimacy of Love

Joy and suffering. Love will never be perfect.

My Heart is a Little Bit Broken

His words have left me breathless.
He is my partner.
My spiritual practice...
My best friend...
The one whom I trust my heart the most...
My forever...
My soul...

Faint whispers of intuition. This feeling.
A deep knowing in my soul that he did not mirror
my desire.

Already feeling vulnerable with my physical.
Menopause at my doorstep. Hormones flowing
endlessly into stories of not good enough.

I do not comprehend the words he has just spoken to
me.

My thoughts
become
unchained and
wild.
Questioning my
very core.

Ugly.
Old.
Unworthy.
Used.
I can do better than you.

I do not know what to do with this information. Truly I do not know what to do.
I am bewildered.

I have always felt an authentic love for him. Pure. Untouched by jealousy and others.

My emotional, spiritual self was safe with him. He held me with compassion and kindness.

Telling me he had never loved anyone as he had loved me.
Telling me our love is the rarest.
Telling me I am his breath.

Was our love an illusion?

My heart is a little bit broken.

I held him on a pedestal. He was like no other.

Now he is just a man.

If You Only Knew

I feel invisible. Unseen by you.
My youth is hidden by my wrinkles.

I can see it in your eyes.
The beauty of younger women overwhelms you like
an aphrodisiac. Always looking elsewhere.

Not at me.
I am here.
Right in front of you.

You are no longer attracted to me. So, you have told
me.

I remember when you would gaze upon me with
desire. Awestruck by my physical presence. A
sensual energy between you and me.

A faint memory now.

I thought I meant more to you.
How foolish and naïve of me. To trust that you would
not betray me with your reckless truth.
I just cry.
Who am I now if I am not admired for my looks?

Lost
Sad

Aging is unfamiliar to me.

The Mirroring of Our Souls

The moment my eyes fell upon you,
I knew.

Your soul whispering a familiar dance,
I knew.

The stillness of your presence unfolding magically in front of me,
I knew.

How beautiful I felt as your smile echoed joy,
I knew.

Words not spoken aloud but a heart singing sweet notes of passion,
I knew.

Your kind truth illuminates my being,
I knew.

Together on this path our souls destined to be,
I knew.

We are not perfection.

Our dark shadows peering through our joy at times.
I see you.

I do not turn away.

Leaning into you. Beyond the fear.

I hear you.

Trust that I will keep you safe.

A sacred space belonging to only you and me.

For this is love.

The mirroring of our souls.

True Love

You say you are broken.
I see a beautiful soul standing before me.

Vulnerable.
Not hiding beyond the shadows.
Breathing his feelings aloud to me.

How can I judge you?

I love you. I love you.

Flawless is what I see.

Pure.
Without any agenda but to love me in return.

Always challenging me to exist at my highest good.

You are joy.
You are compassion.
You are kindness.

This journey of ours is ever evolving….

When Our Souls Met

I am standing beside you in a crowded room.
Do you feel that?

A fiery current racing through my body.

Spiritual.
Sensual
Kind.
Compassionate.

I am breathless.

Do you feel that?

Pure joy.

You look at me with a telling gaze.
You do feel this.

Our souls meet….

A Quiet Heart

Forsaken by my true love.

Not ready to share my vulnerability to yet another.

Standing alone in this moment.

It is calm.

A stillness of being.

I am enjoying this gift of solitude.

My heart is quiet to love.

Chapter 10:
True Beauty is Flawless

A kind heart illuminating the world with every step it takes, connecting with all beings, creatures, and mother earth.

Playful, joyous, and soulful.

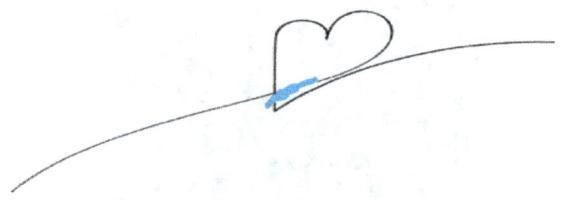

Can you see me?

Truly see me.
I feel invisible to you.
You talk about beauty as if it is skin shallow.
Flawless skin, a youthful glow, Eurocentric features, ageless. I am bewildered.
I do not possess any of these qualities.

My body does not resemble an hourglass, a pear, or any other fruit. Why does my body have to resemble anything?
Are we not all aging from the time we are born? You tell me to be ageless. I hesitate.

The truth is....

It is damning to believe we are only our physical.

Creating self-hatred.
Judging one another.

These meaningless ideas of beauty.
I will not be bound to your false beliefs.

See me.
Truly look into my soul. Beyond the superficial.

Pure and Untouchable.

Unconditional love of self.

This is my beauty.

Illusions of the Face

To exist in this world's ideals of beauty is what I desperately crave. I need to be seen but not deeply.

Superficial layers of skin and body bound, tweaked, pulled, exercised, lasered, injected, knifed into perfection.

My time spent tirelessly creating the idyllic femininity. Not quite there.

Always something hindering my efforts of excellence. I am determined.

I know I will be perfectly beautiful one day.

There is just this one thing….
A faint whisper from deep within.

It has always been present since my childhood.
I have tried my best to silence it with distractions.
Never leaving me, it speaks its truth with compassion and kindness.

"You are perfect, just as you are, in this very moment."

Truth be told, I am tired.

All my life and now I am middle aged.
Not quite there.

This dream of an ideal femininity is destructive.
I have neglected so many aspects of myself.

I do want to be deeply seen.
See me beneath my skin and body.

My true self.

My Buddha Nature. Aware, loving, and wise.
The illusion of the face is momentary.
My Buddha Nature is eternal.

Chapter 11: The Mindfulness of Children

Children Are Our Teachers.

Children: Living Life in This Moment

Whenever I am in the presence of children, I am hopeful. Encouraged that we can live in a harmonious world.

Confident that the exchange of words between beings is created from a place of loving kindness and truth.

Their joyous laughter and authentic smiles create an energy of gratitude.

Happily running and skipping around this earth with no destination in sight.

Living from a place of fearlessness.

Liberated.

Free of ego and self-judgment.

Existing in this moment.

What strength they possess to be their genuine selves. Children are our best teachers on living mindfully. Just take some moments to observe them in their daily lives. It is a wondrous example of just being.

Children: Living Life in This Moment

A reminder of where we came from and what we can return to.

Our Buddha Nature...

Chapter 12: The Joy of Writing

Uninhibited.
Liberated.
This is my voice.

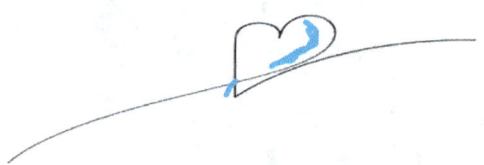

Just like Poetry

As my path of mindfulness and meditation evolves,
I move towards you with awareness and love.

I am not a separate self.
Can you feel this deep belonging?
Our sufferings and joys are no different.

Nevermore riding the waves of isolation. Nevermore detaching ourselves from one another.

I cannot deny this truth....

Our nature is pure like gold.
Unattainable by the ego.

Wisdom from within.

Gazing into your soul, I see myself.

Compassion
Love

Just like poetry,
We are the essence of beauty and truth.

Knowing

To live in fear, I do not.

   Never
agitation.

   No
limitation.

   Only
Compassion.

My heart expands with love.

   Truth unfolds endlessly.

     Guided by my beloved,
       Buddha Nature.

         A quiet knowing.

As Life Unfolds

As life unfolds,

The illusion of perfection we pretend to embrace unravels.

The untruths we hide behind crumble.

The identities we craft out of fear disappear.

The relationships we cling to weaken.

The absence of self-love from our own hearts fade.

Spiraling into chaos.

It is messy.
It is dark.
It is painful.

A death of what we believed to be our true existence.

We can push back. Fight. Defend what was once ours.

But…
life will not stop unfolding its truth.

To choose to lean into this messiness?

Unraveling layers of old wounds and pain.
This is the journey of liberation.

It is difficult to fathom such a path.

You are not alone. It is the human experience.

Always embraced by compassion and loving kindness.

The unfolding of life.

Dedication

To my teachers who have embraced me with loving kindness, compassion, and wisdom.

To my parents who love only as a mother and father can.

To my intimate circle of friends, you challenge me to live at my highest good.

To my mindfulness practice, I could never be without.

And

To my soulmate,

My heart is filled with you.
Our souls are drawn together in each lifetime.
You are the embodiment of all that is sweet and pure.

Who is Kim Nicole

Living in compassion and loving kindness, being humane to ourselves and mother earth is powerful and can only result in goodness for us all.

Kim's practice of mindfulness and meditation has been a journey of self-discovery and profound healing. Learning how to skillfully turn towards the challenges of life with kindness and compassion has transformed her life. Excited to share her experiences through mindfulness poetry, Kim hopes she can be a support to others on their path of spiritual awakening.

Kim is a Licensed Master Social Worker with over 15 years of experience in this field. Enjoying a long-time practice of yoga, Kim holds a 500 RYT certification. A seeker of kind wisdom, Kim recently graduated from the 2-year Mindfulness Meditation Teacher Certification Program created by Jack Kornfield and Tara Brach.

Kim has always lived the life of a wanderer from a young age. Growing up in a military family, the need to travel and learn about other cultures has never left her. Kim has had residence in the United States, United Arab Emirates, and now Asia. Who knows where she will be a year from now!

Kim enjoys writing poetry, living her practice of mindfulness and yoga, and traveling the world re-discovering herself at each turn of life.

LIVE FULLY IN EACH MOMENT

www.ingramcontent.com/pod-product-compliance
Lightning Source LLC
LaVergne TN
LVHW022000060526
838201LV00048B/1642